Red Blood Black Ink White Paper
New and Selected Poems 1961 ~ 2001

Red Blood Black Ink White Paper
❖*New and Selected Poems*❖
1961 ~ 2001

Phyllis Gotlieb

TORONTO

Exile Editions
2002

This edition is published by Exile Editions Limited,
20 Dale Avenue, Toronto, Ontario, Canada   M4W 1K4

Sales Distribution:
McArthur & Company
c/o Harper Collins
1995 Markham Road
Toronto, ON
M1B 5M8
toll free:
1 800 387 0117
(fax) 1 800 668 5788

Design, Composition by TIM HANNA
Cover Design by ZERO WEATHER
Typeset at MOONS OF JUPITER INC.
Author Photograph by JOHN REEVES
Printed and Bound at AGMV MARQUIS

THE CANADA COUNCIL | LE CONSEIL DES ARTS
FOR THE ARTS | DU CANADA
SINCE 1957 | DEPUIS 1957

ONTARIO ARTS COUNCIL
CONSEIL DES ARTS DE L'ONTARIO

The publisher wishes to acknowledge
the assistance toward publication of
the Canada Council and the Ontario Arts Council.

ISBN 1-55096-601-4

*In
Memory
of
Margaret Ford*

❖Contents❖

From **Dr. Umlaut's Earthly Kingdom** ❖*1974*

From **The Works** ❖*1978*

Selected Later Poems

Mirror

The grasshopper with his complex
of triggered legs protects
the pulsing essence
of his mobled thorax;

behind the incandescence
sungift on his
blackdrop eyes emergence
snicks and pries
ichor, green brackish liquor

from clapperclawed
greenstiff blades, he
darts, the fencer
nipping sincerely;

sunstationed on bricks, trusts
me who thirsts
for elixirs and defecting
from stone halls of Time reflects
the grasshopper with his complex

Aquarius

The slow clock whorls of snails
mark time here; such calendars
patterned earlier dark ooze
into reluctant longitudes.

Fluted they give lipservice
over sand and slime,
dance, hornbranching
one-footed sine
impervious

while molly and platy
(bread-and-butter names)
nip-nap-nubble the grown scrolls
of snailshell, gossip the green.

Behind the screen
of glass I watch,
scrape algae, dole
dry crumbs of food into the gape
of tiger-striped predators,
a blaze of jaws untoothed

still showing in memory of the warmer
Amazon (a lunge and seethe
of living waters) the red raw gorge.

Beyond these elegant admirations
in the pale fishwarmth of antichlorined waters
frilly snails pace
poring glissandos sucklocked
to glass, timeless, the protozoan's
relentless ungrace.

Day Falcon

The falconer of the Sun
holds the day's tiercel
hooded at the twilight band
imperious for the morsel
of shadow and starshine;

nervous they stand:

wrist-heavy with pride
the prey-bird of morning
waits for the sign.

Now! Loose hood and jess!

With spring and thrust
of great claws on the wrist
and the wind singing of wings
leaving his master
arm-branded still
with the bracelet of touch,

wheeling and turning
high and faster
with the mark of his going
written on the sky
through covert and meadow
he scours out the shadow
with the light of his eye!

The falconer hoods the
eye, cruel and blazing,
and every dark shred dropped from the claws
(of night and the covert, cool rich dews
grass couches of lovers
the quick eye of the fox
and the sweet grazing of all wild things) withers
on glittering rocks
and the cold veneer or rivers
into flickering mist;

and the falconer shivers
with the lust of his pride
but the hawk's urge is dead
and he sleeps on the wrist.

A Cocker of Snooks

We kept him an hour in the
bottom of a bushel basket, a
flourish fit for a john hancock, not particularly
brainy, his trowelhead
narrower than the lithe surprising
bulk, like a stretchsock holds
any size frog or toad *blip*
the red tongue, in hand skinshabby
the snake ideal of boneplate
hidden, he needed a new
coat or maybe a dose of
Plantshine, but released
he turned into grassblade leaf stone twig
blip the red tongue said, *that*
for you! he
owed us nothing but the grace of God.

The Young Dionysus

The quick essential track of the
rabbit on the white cover
chief of the snow
remarks here and
there where he
leaped, turned, fled

the great scarifying
boots of the bullyboys
who cry hunt Euhoi! harsh
Bacchic call in the morning
airs of the young

        the rabbit
himself transcendent invisible
godlike in absence having unaccountably
marked this pale augury an
hour before sunrise.

Matinée

The monkey stops his
to-and-fro to the chain's end only
to toss off a trick
with a back flip arrogant
as a Spanish grandee, in body
slender and muscular, a
tempered coil on the chance
a link may snap
               cocking
the narrow cynic eye

his honed critical face set against
the pushback bowler and pocky nose of his man, he
signals
with the sprung whorl of his tail: I'm on
a chain, but by God I keep it taut.

Retroactive

A handful of snow crumbles
to temper the wine;
Come, says Pliny, drink my fine
cold (faintly sunspiced) mead
with sweet cake, oh, and a lettuce for every man
bittersweet between the teeth (I read between the lines) besides
three snails and two eggs
and the fine black pearls of olives. Look up from the dregs
at that table where you've propped your sickened head
bellyful of oysters, earsful of the clangour
of dancing-girls from Cadiz, and remember
next time to eat at Pliny's.

A handful of snow

melts. Take care, Pliny—
now you are in your cups
of honeymead—when you go
climbing Vesuvius, to see what's in the crater
don't venture too far
or like the fly in amber
end pressed in the crisping ember.

No more white porches of sunwashed stone
for you, olives, onions and wine,
the mouthstings of memory: ashes on the charred teeth,
hands clasped on the curious man's pick and mallet
and silence.

       If no mind recalls it but mine,
I'll say: Pliny, if I remember it, memory will tremble
on Everyman's dead palate.

a handful of snow

Frontal Cumulus

Under the eaves of the storm voices rise
more piercing and echo down
from the cloudlid. Funeral
bells toll toiling knifegrinder tattershoe
down roads, torn felt hat pulled over
the face by Hieronymus Bosch.

Children don't watch for him, black and grey
man weatherburned mediaeval dun, his
mind a grind of knifesparks
under the grey felt hat, colour of cloud
eyes the colour of lightning.

Caveat Emptor

Before the rain comes down the red bricks glare
frank gaping hellmouths between mortar lines
grasses stand rigid as the spines
of an arched cat's back in the nervous air
and silver sided leaves burn in a rare
oxygen of electricity;
the changeling light wavers undersea
pattern of glaucous dusk and ominous pearl.

The rolling reds and grey thunderous greens
colours Milton saw in his blind's eye
and painted hell with, etch the memory
of sound and sorrow, pass the cloudy lens
and subtle pulsing humours in a camera
impossible to tell truth from chimaera.

Similetics

TIRETRACKS

      in snow
thread filet popcorn picot
lace on bobbin
wheeled roads
      unwinding
white swags complicate
crystalline simplicities
           as witness
in the pure fields: footprints
drop catspaw doilies trim
as a spinster's parlour, stars
turned antimacassars.

GARDENER

      goes by, a
bent sickle, 2 pepsi
empties swing (wine's gone)
over the weeds, he plans
hoeing the parsley; his
earth shirt bends low, cross white
gallus X marks the spot
where the heart is, the
whizzbang watch on his wrist keeps
one time, the cooling sun
another.

STARFOOT

         the grave girls
hop, scotch
on chalks mark knurled
asphalt
         in evening sky
change; go map the
constellations where Dipper-
fingered they
cast a last
stone (meteor)

Small World

Boys play with marbles that catch
the fire and centre of the star
and planetary Catseyes swarm
round the great Boulder they adore.

The dirty hand snapfingers
taut english to conjure
Pureys, their heliocentric clash
and magisterial furor.

Afternoons, SEAGRAMS blazes
on knee-swung bags, by scabby
shins, catch-suns they jangle
the imprisoned galaxies.

Latitude

Mercator a map
maker a shaper
of great currents of
continents on paper

seen from whatever
angle resembled
a tangle of embryos
half-formed reassembled

near strangled by
circulus equinoctialis
tropicus capricorni, swaddling
bands of a terra infantilis

born out of theodolite
imagination
and the declivity of
faint constellation

grown to surprising
stature? on paper
by nature a proper
tantrumtaker!

Kylix Krater Amphora

Small men like deer with winedark eyes
crisp hair and skins of amber
paint black on terra cotta
:for export only
:to the victor belong the oils
for some rich Etruscan lip to roll
in grease along the krater's rim.

Small men with tongues like bees
moist brushes flicklicking
lips may kiss kylix
never; arched dolphins
swarm: branching
deer graze always here in the utmost
calm. Exekias

himself points the finger, scratches
at the untrue line. Shards
grate under his sandals *fool*
Brown hands of the small men lift for his mark tenderly
the figured
amphora.

Haiku on Brueghel

burning on the snow
drag-footed across the fields
whiskey-faced men go

the blind lead the blind
and coarse oglers invade the
countries of the mind

Icarus falling
makes what mark on the seas where
wild birds are calling

can children who play
a thousand multicoloured
games be dead today?

Hospitality

Da Vinci and the man on the bed stare
at each other through the dark air of
death watch. The dying man more than half
suspects from the black glitter
beneath the eaved brows that it is Death
watching;

       Da Vinci moodily
hones in his mind the silver
saw he has made to trepan the skull.

Three Dutch Paintings

I

lines around a picture

oysters and lemons. speak to me of love.
the shining flagon mirrors the unknown window
looking out through the mind's lens.
naked and peeled the crystal yellow planes
of lemon seen even as you and eye.
speak of love. that lemons were such jewels.
oysters so phlegmy. so yesterday you saw them.
dead today. so I see today.
tomorrow dead.
betrayer.
you have stopped my mouth with clay.

II

interior

roomy room rooms of checkerboard tile
opening into nothing into nothing nothing into
boxing the porcelain pearly cheeked girls
twisting and twining the pearly cheeked pearls

rerereading the crumplecrumped letter
kissing or delousing the child as choice has it
chaos contorted informed and incorporated and
imitated beyond nothing.

III

eripuit persona

Rembrandt Harmenszoon van Rijn
I know you by the guise you're in:
the spirit's dress from youth to age
compassionate in pilgrimage.

Rembrandt Harmenszoon van Rijn
    lover of Saskia and Hendrijcke
    Titus, ponds, windmills
    rings and ruffs of burghers
    seduced by Ganymede
    Samson embattled and every weary
    prophet with scuffed sandal

I know you by the guise you're in
    Rembrandt, you rosy youth with gold-wire hair
    sowing those lines in tender joy and patience
    till your face has flowered with
    each promised bud of love and death;

the spirit's dress from youth to age
    painter and etcher of the lines in that face
    both from within and without
    and with every arabesque of gold helmet
    lighting and enlightening the eyes beneath
    in the Dutch and sun-mote afternoon of Rembrandt

compassionate in pilgrimage.

Trompe l'Oeil

Hokusai hoped the almond-eyed
ladies would step down and share his
tea. He crouched over grainy paper
abstract, waiting for
a sting of his crinkled
seas to mark his skin
                          and men
brought him money in twists of paper more
dimensional than the
quivering waterfalls silvering his
pages.
        I see him there,
brown-eyed and indignant.

Brueghel's Day

In the morning, children come bellowing from burrows
steamheated holes in the wall, extrusions
of wood and steel unfolding, wagons
tricycles, playpens, enamelled
heliotropes of noon.

Day reverberates with them in beaten gongs of wall and sky
Brueghel-coloured and intense.

Hard-bodied, hot, they shrill past zenith
turning and burning fleshflamed, crying
out against dark with the candour of the sun
they cannot stop

till that misty verge, the Corot-time
claims them to bed where bodies
still taut give off clear
candleheat from their fierce metabolisms

and outside all the lawn and sidewalk day has folded
except where the classic line of a velocipede
standing stern as a heraldic dog
sable on vert, waits for the rust of night.

Polyhedron

Dry foxfalls of padded feet go prowling
round and round the hentracks of my mind,
my knotted, night-nodding head;
rheum-red eyes, kerosene flares cry Danger!
nose crimped to the acrid smell
mouth an orifice of doom-
warning to

.children.

go scouring vacant lots, toe-turning
bright green shards of shattered glass
beerbottles (boys, we've had a bellyful)
Scytheman whispers: love 'em and leave 'em
boys, and leave 'em

.widows.

live in empty houses with clocks that go CLINK CLANK
refrigerators that rattle NOT NOW
and dry footfalls that whisper never

time dusts the mantelpiece
and the mirrors grieve
(R.I.P.) clichés.

A Table of Passions

Imagine in the baby's span of head
enreeled the miles of neuron tracks
and ask what fool living or dead
calls it a tablet of scraped wax.

The coming attraction, sex
enmeshed in flickering trajectories, zone to zone
pulled by fierce raptures of the breast
into the woof of love; not alone:

a thousand grandparents lie buried
bonemeal to feed the seed of name
lawgivers mark with the same
calipers each unvirgined feature;

unmarked by stylus the creature
of my face and yours forever married
in one body, the marvel
of passions waiting to be opened
no dictum may unravel.

Seventh Seal

Gauntface or madshadow tell
me what the world is? I know
years at the Sat. Mat.
aft in the Loges, I learned
Injuns come
                    triggerspring
lovespurned.
                    The tears of Kings
are glycerine. With salt I
salute them.
                    The curly shirlies
taught us the innocent bit
Stars in the screenlit
eyes flickered, wanderers
rode westering, broad as a
barndoor and dumb
with virtue;
                    oh, how we watched
horsekiss the cassidy come
to THE (sunset) END till they
forced us unhatched
pupas into the white
bitter late Saturday light.

Lost Unfound

My father's managing a theatre was
how we got our umbrellas, shabby
late-thirties flappers, musty
feathered winging down ribrusted
denizens in our timid zoo
of savaged wallets and thinned
wedding-bands unclaimed
by pathos
        but I sat in the
lumber-room among NOW SHOWING signs
reading creased letters, marvels in
disdained purses:
do you love me, Mabel?
                not a pennysworth, Joe

troves I lost I never looked for: cracked
fountain pens that stained my fingers wastened
by irreconcilable degrees into
the dust.

Late Gothic

From the window of my grandfather's
front room above the store I could see
over the asylum wall through the barred window
a madwoman raving, waving
pink arm sleeves. From the kitchen at the back
faceted skylights lay, grown quartz among the sooty
stalagmite chimneys. Two faces of despair.

My grandmother and grandfather cultivated
in the scoured yard of their love
a garden of forget-me.

My grandmother was a golden
turbulence, my goldwin, giver of all
lovehated vortex. Like all children I looked
twenty-five years later at her picture and found
the woman, monstrously coarse and obese
a drowned reaching beauty.

My grandfather, crumpled old Jew, read Hebrew
through a magnifying glass, crawled
to the park for sun, swore, told old tales
babbled of green fields and died.

My father sold that legendary
furniture for twelve dollars
                          and we smelled the stench
of the furs the old man had made his shapeless coats of
and went down the narrow walled stair for the last time
into the bright street between the wall upflung
against the howling chimney of the madwoman's throat
on the one side
and the redbrick rampart of shoddy stores against the
reaching blackened arms of the chimneys on the other.

Marble Zodiac

Metamorphosis struck midnight: the Scales stopped their balancing act
Aquarius dropped his buckets and tried to scratch his stone head
Ram looked for a barn door to butt and broke his Parian horn
Bleated and kicked Capricorn, who
Leaped and came down dangerously cracked; the Fishes
Eyed each other with their usual unconcern

Zing! went the last of the Archer's arrows
Over the sky; the Lion roared and was silent; Virgo
Didn't change much: she was always cold; the Crab turned
Into a scarab, a very decorative, so did Scorpio
And the Twins closed their eyes, forgot the primal Egg; and the Bull
Chuffed, pawed once with a stiff leg and thought: I'm growing old

(Note: some years ago, when a group of my poems appeared in *The Canadian Forum*, Milton Wilson, then one of the editors, remarked absent-mindedly in a biographical note that Phyllis Gotlieb had published a book of verse called MARBLE ZODIAC. I replied with the above; it appeared in the *Forum* next issue.)

A Commentary

Good morning, the old man says
good morning toward the
yeshiva in heavystep
bookbag clasping
books in black letters blacker
than the ovens of Auschwitz lettershapes
crimped round thought/tongues of fire
his eyes are
wetstones
his beard splayed, in shoe heavystep
he smokes, breathes, breathsmoke
pillars the air
good morning:
melamed,

on Saturday morning
melamed, good Shabbas, he
brings home a minyan
of Hasidim for l'chaim

l'chaim!

in black :
caftans, fur streimlach : white
stockings : swung sidecurls :
pink flesh : black
asphalt green leaves : yellow sunlight blue
sky they come
step : walk
in a black flock pass

from pane to pane black
brown pink white black brown pink
white betweengreen
aisles of glass

when I go by the school where
minds may be narrowed I see
the yard a hundred Jewish children
laugh yell and raise hell
red blue green yellow

eyes like washed stones
splayed beard, a bringer of Hasidim
spreads the leaves of his prayers for them
: *this is an aleph*
his children have succumbed to Cyclon B

the old man smiles
good morning

good morning!
         from Lubavichi, Lublin
Bratzlav, Berditchev : Berlin
from Modzitz, Mezrich, Bialystock
Fastov, Opatov, Lodmir, Lodz

: *ghostmarch in the noon of night*
from pane to pane black brown pink white
betweengreen
aisles of glass

The Child the Tchelitchew the Tree

hide & seek
says Tchelitchew, the world's
a dandelion's eye
the hand child branches the
embryo root, red
shining head and

one, two, three
says Tchelitchew, the
child's the tree

balanced between fear and
joy, the shapes
of children turn the tree
from sun to earth and back
a lattice dark/day/light

I spy
with my eye
how the night
pulls down the sky

I stayed three nights
beside her bed
don't let the moon
touch me, she said

and Tchelitchew said, I eschew
the cold blue
pigment of the moon

(because he knew
the tree of bone)

there is no terror here, says
Tchelitchew, you do not know
that does not lace your vision's vein
your vascular
privateflowered tree

and he chose red and yellow
skybluepink & green

one, two, three
,Peggy Lee
sing a rainbow in a tree

the hand hides, but the child
pushes through dandelion-
eyed, preposterously red
blueveined embryonic head
to bring the light, to salt the tree
to be the word against the dead

In the Lablight

the embryos in jars
have sad imprisoned faces
though they are beyond wars
naughtmen inside walls
they have no navels, only
roughcut umbilicals

dream not under the kind
amnion but the moon
of the eye's microtome
knives will extrude their causes
neither tide nor wind
move them, not even
nightmare; they have no marvels

So Long It's Been

time to clear the silent
sullen round of numbers stacked in my
brainracks
            clear HOWARD 0141 where the one
armed man lived next door and Mrs Goldfarb
with her slipstraps slid on her fat pink arms
                                    clear
HARGRAVE 8375 where the park sweeps below the railing
and Broadview Ave, on a foggy day a ship's
deck sailing a sea of limbo washed with
3 old skaters 7 tennis players and a shattered
rubbydub
            GERRARD 6715 Good evening Century Theatre

Goodbye Mrs Gersten, Miss Fernandez, Miss Fleuhrer &
all burglars anonymous uncaught who tied up my
father & stole the safe, or his lunch, or sometimes
even $$$$
            clear GERRARD 2222 (too) easy to remember *call
me anytime* Mr Wallace walks me in the schoolyard &
knowing does not tell me my grandmother
                              LAKESIDE 0007
never liked flowers because they reminded her of
funerals: how many roses from hers have I found
cracking the backs of Uncle Nissel's
SCHUYLER 4-7767 old encyclopedias?
                        clear GROVER 9595
where I pulled the kid cousin's braids, ate
knishes, and cried: yes, he's dead, he died this
morning
            numbers that lived in me clear clear clear no
answer, nobody lives
there any more

A Picnic of Pedants

etymology's words
                    entomology
bugs. near as no difference, ant
looks a word, quarters
leaves, carries
weight.
          centipede a very
myriapod
            maybe dip a
spider in ink and produce
calligraphy, if you prefer
or
pick a word: for instance
etymology unlimber-
ing curly legs
and and and and and and and
scrawling across this page

Sub Rosa

I don't know why, but robins choose
our crazy trellis-fence for the house
beautiful; stick straw string mud anything
goes, motherbird
deeps it with her bronze
burnisher; the secret hours out
4 copper sulphate globes kids
palm in sweaty hatchery while she
heads for the wormfront; one falls,
one vanishes, 2 wet nurslings break
shell, kids bear away empty
prizes, catspaw the begonias, fledglings
barbaric yawp earth & sky, kids
lift them, leave enriched
breadcrumbs in the murphy bed, motherbird
climbs the sunbeam, careless
as a mechanical
nightingale but
somehow
one
puffed
broody speckled
as an egg and ovoid youngster
survives kids going kitchycoo
and his cold bed, sums up the lot
                              become
thrice bigger than his dam, hangs around the
kitchen in his striped sweater, gulping
a slug now & then, a lubberly
caliban; well, she's
no momist, heaves the lout
over the side, he shrieks! scrunches in nakedeye
beam of the sun snivelling
for a soft featherwing of his ma, hops
here & there, weeps, noplacetogo, we chase
the fluffy lummox all round our yard
and the neighbour's scared of dogs, find
him a fencepost

                    trembles
grieves you'll-be-sorry, makes excuses, wets
his foot in the air and gets off
the pad at last;
                      merrywidow having flown the
coop lies open to the wandering
cuckoo

In Season

I watch
        chameleons and
children, children and
chameleons: one
elegant appetite sheds
skin every three weeks or
so, slits
seam on his tooth edge
spine bump grind and
shimmies around till he
stands loosened in the trans-
lucent shimmy of his own skin
shoots cuff sloughs grabbing
with claw, gobbles it
down to save protein and swift
flick-switches to try out
the same brown/green he started
with
        children
writhing yearning and striving
hoicked up by jerky inches
measured wristbare and pantsleg
put out rawbone joint sweat gland
sex stirring trying to sow miracles
without seed casing the raw still
power, bust
clothes knee elbow & prat &
jettison ragged shirt, wracked
shoe leaving of outcast
armories
        how pectoral grooves the steel
breastplate shapes of the warm

skin form them
        in season I watch
them outgrow my arms

Three Translations of Villon

1. PROVERBS

Enough butting, you bust your head
enough dipping, the pitcher breaks
enough firing, the iron turns red
enough hammering, you get cracks
enough running and you make tracks
enough goodness, you'll pull out plums
enough naughtiness, you get smacks
enough calling and Christmas comes

enough talking and you'll raise doubt
enough fame and you'll find the claques
enough promises, you'll back out
enough wishing, maybe it takes
enough boozing, you get the shakes
enough starving, you gobble crumbs
enough gobbling, your belly aches
enough calling and Christmas comes

enough howling, you feed the mutt
enough buzzing and you'll make wax
enough keeping, the apples rot
enough picking and you'll break locks
enough dithering, your luck croaks
enough hurry and you're all thumbs
enough betting, you lose the stakes
enough calling and Christmas comes

enough nagging, you should drop dead
enough spending, you're on the rocks
enough kindness, you're out of bread
enough promises won't mend socks
enough faith will move bricks and blocks
enough lending, you'll beg for dimes
enough blowing will blow down oaks
enough calling and Christmas comes

Prince: enough humbling, a fool chokes
enough living, what's left of dreams?
enough rope—there's no time for jokes!
enough calling and Christmas comes

2. Ein Breve Tsu Zein Chaverim

Won't anybody have pity on me?
can't you hear me out there any of you?
friends I'm depending on? jump in the sea!
Stuck in a ditch! What did I ever do
to deserve you—yes you, tearing a shoe
with the Hasidim; try it here, instead
and you'll find out! Long as your belly's fed
and you pick up a penny here and there
maybe you think I'm on a featherbed?
I ask you, can you leave me lying here?

It's so dark you could go blind; who can see
through stone walls? the quiet's like deafness; blue
sky and wind mean nothing to you: you're free—
I'm a bone in the bottom of a stew
pot, a fly buzzing in a pot of glue;
you're home guzzling borsht till your beards are red
—and my beard's red with blood! you're stuffing bread
and bagels: sure, you'll boil me chickens, sure,
you'll make me soup with farfel—when I'm dead!
I ask you, can you leave me lying here?

Come on, if you have any decency,
look what I'm in, here, and if you're not too
busy gnawing the toothpick, bring a key.
I get a crust that every time I chew
it, I lose a tooth, when they want to know
something they don't ask me nicely, they flood
my gut with water . . . I'm already glad
Tuesdays when they make me a Yom Kippur
and also Fridays . . . hungry, cold, afraid
I ask you, can you leave me lying here?

Tsarevitch, if you do the will of God
please let me go! The others let me bleed.
They're worse than pigs. Pigs, at least, if they hear
one squeal, they all come running . . . do I need
to beg you? Will you leave me lying here?

❖Red Blood Black Ink White Paper

3. SMALL TALK

I know how milk gets full of flies
I know apples fall near the tree
I know the weather by the skies
I know men by their vanity
I know the honey from the bee
I know the worker from the drone
I know you can't get off scot free
I know all spirits but my own

I know some lovers by their sighs
I know some jackets by their fleas
I know some thieves with shifty eyes
I know monks by their rosaries
I know nuns by their modesties
I know good wine by cask and tun
I know when fools are full of cheese
I know all spirits but my own

I know how pigs live in their sties
I know how fish come from the sea
I know two bits and what it buys
I know Matilda and Marie
I know of sleep and fantasy
I know the Pope, I know the Throne
I know of faith and heresy
I know all the spirits but my own

Prince, I know all diversity
I know the flesh, I know the bone
I know how death will feed on me
I know all spirits but my own

I Ask You

Suppose Catullus had lived on and on
an aging boy, never quite growing up?
always sure of a jug to fill the cup
a hand to pour it and a redeye dawn?
supposing Keats had married Fanny Brawne
shrugged off TB and in a chemist's shop
while the harsh tinctures gathered drop by drop
dreamed a new wild way-out Endymion?

and if Byron had come back from his war
and written I WAS THERE and SEE IT NOW
would ancient toothless Burns, pushed to the edge
by fifty women, long for the lost plough?
would roaring Brendan meekly sign the pledge?
and Dylan, sobered down, take up guitar?

❖Red Blood Black Ink White Paper

A Discourse

the skeleton's the most articu-
late thing there is except
about Who made him. It's not
graveyards he rattles in but
you and me; skeletons
chase butterflies and do the
Monster Mash in the dark infra-
redroom of the flesh

                    starting
from the grounded arches of
Man's first pedestal the
Tarsals and Phalanges bones
baby needs shoes for, not
the ones that get them,
keystones for

                legs of
concern to dashers and prancers
stylers and milers fencers fandancers
romancers advancers
and retreaters
                unsinewed a collection
of bones named after
skillets and safety pins

                the Femur
the skeleton's oaktree, in the old
soon broken least mended
has little to recommend it
in a poem except in the thunderclaptrap
of one lowly notch called the Intercondylar
and one lordly knob called the Greater Trochanter

while Pelvis itself ugly needs flesh
to notify it yet a crown of bones
in the woman the royal
colander drains
life from the sea
waters of the uterine cavern

and
the tailbone, Coccyx well
named after the cuckoo
connects with old jokes of banana
peels but the Pelvis
attaches that column of latin
the spine, at the Sacrum

in form
eschew connotations of
ramrod or spinelessness, choose
for symbol the integral,
S- shaped,both practical and pleasing; here are
integers stacked like
lecture chairs but cushioned in use
always; muscles may atrophy but these
let heads held high
glare each other in the eye
and swear

rising out of lumbago country and its young
ambassador absorbine junior
through thorax the Dorsals
seem to belong to dolphins
rather than the ribcage
called cavity crammed with vitals

the seven bars of the neck
noted for the top two that help
you nod or shake
so superbly lubricated only
the heart goes creak

the Hyoid hangs out
in this district, a bone
without visible means of support
silent and anonymous in
the mugbook of the anatomist

but the arms have apparatus!
clefshaped Clavicle
doubles the spine's integral
over the stave of the Ribs most
graceful of all body
spans from Sternum to Scapula a
flat plate and the base of wings in angels
armsocket in Mankind;

the humerus: enough said;

Radius and Ulna are staff and support
for that fan that pinwheel that unbeached
starfish the hand: I think of arms raised
lotus columns of Egypt
buttressed by shouldermuscle
and finally fingers touching tips
over the Skull, full
circle from the Phalanges we began with

the Skull's the pontine
arch of the pontifex homely
to me, the only one I met

in person, as a child
                    my medschool
cousin used a sawed-off
skulltop for ashtray I thought
the flakes inside were dried remains
of brains, bonepink shocked me reading
so much of desert alkali but knew
the concave brainshape volutes cup
cortex and arteriole

                    when
you put your lefthand
fingers into the inter-
stices of your right is how
the Frontal fits the Parietals
in the noble Cranium the base
doesn't look that neat
but none the less suffices

                    the
Ethmoid takes the weight
of the great oracle with its flutes and coils
Temporals remind us
how bound to time we are Zygomatics
give children those apple
cheeks
            leave Sphenoid
Conchae, Palatines all fragile none
termed ephemeral for

Stapes, Malleus, Incus
the Auditory Ossicles a
tone poem of their own tell you
what goes bump in the night, usually
the kid falling out of bed on his
Occiput

from here the Foramen Magnum opens the door
from the brain to the neural telegraph
lines strung along the vascular
tree in lands I have no visa for

balled in a burlap of triple
membranes the rooty
brain's a thing contained and only
container of everything best left
cased under the lock and key of its senses

bridge span arch imply
traffic
        in the complex I
admire most the Foramina piercing
bone where marrow hatching phagocytes knock on the wall
arcades where nerve and vein pass through
providentially
and begin to define the flesh

the spirit's limits have their arbiters
but I know where the devil
starts

Death's Head

at 3 a.m. I run my tongue
around my teeth (take in a breath)
(give out a breath) take one more step
approaching death. my teeth are firm
and hard and white (take in a breath)
incisors bite and molars grind
(give out a breath) the body lying
next to mine is sweet and warm
I've heard that worms (take in a breath)
don't really eat (give out a breath)
the coffin meat of human kind
and if they did I wouldn't mind
that's what I heard (take in a breath)
(and just in time) I think it's all
a pack of lies. I know my flesh
will end in slime. the streets are mean
and full of thieves. the children in
the sleeping rooms (give out a breath)
walk narrowly upon my heart
the animal beneath the cloth
submerged rises to any bait
of lust or fury, love or hate
(take in a breath) my orbic skull
is eminently frangible
so delicate a shell to keep
my brains from spillage. still my breath
goes in and out and nearer death

and yet I seem to get to sleep

A Ballad of 2 Voices, N.Y.

Aunt Sarah:
I started life on 3rd St.
where whores and perverts flourished
I ran from them on the legs
soup & farfel nourished

Phyllis:
Why is the bearded
man alone with his coat folded neat-
ly on the greengrass bouncing
a ball on the parkpath?

Aunt Sarah:
my mother wore a sheitel
my father wore a tallith
they blinked blind eyes at voyeurs
what did they know of brothels?

Phyllis:
the young browndown counter
man sprouts from his allhands
plate knife fork *zip*!
cups like capuchins leap
from his frondpalms

Aunt Sarah:
my father dug in the subway pit
an immigrant with a barrow
my mother baked pletzlach
and lifted the fallen sparrow

Phyllis:
O am I blessed
(plink)? is a tear
drop from an angel of God
falling on my forehead or
only a drip from an
overhead air conditioner?

Aunt Sarah:
I had a husband, fed
a son who fought in a place
I never heard of; he died
with madness in his face

Phyllis:
young Negro girls go down-
town at a strut, jut-
ting out breast & backside, en-
joying what they've got

Aunt Sarah:
my husband, my son are dead
my parents far buried
I hate the city I loved in
it's an apache I married

Phyllis:
it's the Friedsam
carousel, ringading where I
get my nostalgi@ 2 for 2 bits I'm
putting a clause in my will ring-
ading, for the children of
Time, for the silver and gold
of my love ringading
for the children, the silver
the gold . .

Aunt Sarah:
I was mugged in my own street
I lay like a cursed stone
but I'm tough as the city that grew me
I die by the inch alone.

Pop! Goes the Easel

What happened was
all the fathombeasts that ever bashed
the surface/tension of the
shadowscreen and the silent stealthy shadow
trackers of the killer and the brash ones too the
Bulldog/drummers and Maigret/regretters
Hammers of God/forsaken louts and loonies
King Kongs & Mings of Mongo
came up for air I mean
Pow! right off the page/screen/canvas
alive in simultaneous reality
on this the fairflower of our lambent
earth billboard & boxtop Wow! what
rowwracking nights we had
then, what adrenalin/docked days
running amok the concurrence of walleyed
thieves thugs yeggs mugs spivs till they'd
Docsavaged & Hairsbreadth/harried us, you & me
Bam! onto the page/screen/canvas Greatscott
& Ogeegosh we were

feelin no pain. I mean.
no pain.
no love. Nothing but
flicker & writhe in
2 constrained dimensions no
hailstones gallstones flintstones
were our weather our rage
decalcomania. That's how it crumbled.

Sometimes
they look/read/watch us strange
phenomena of their immaterial
age of ex
crescent dinosaurs & leaping
lizards. And turn away. We stir
no passions, Charley. If they grieve
guiltfingered
Bonds console them. So

kiss me quick before the fade out
out and tell me
in one balloon, one frame
                              the way we
played it, what did we have Toulouse
Lautrec?

Ordinary, Moving

is the name of the game
laughing, talking where the ball bounces
in the forgotten schoolyard
one hand, the other hand; one foot, the other foot
you know the one
(Saturday Afternoon Kid
blackball-cracker, scotchmint-muncher
handkerchief-chewer extraordinary)
clap front, clap back
ballthwack on the boardfence
front and back, back and front
arms of old beeches reaching over drop their
sawtooth leaves in your hair

       (as I was sitting beneath a tree
       a birdie sent his love to me
       and as I wiped it from my eye
       I thought: thank goodness cows can't fly)

tweedle, twydle
curtsey, salute
and roundabout
until you're out

the shadows turn, the light is long
and while you're out you sing this song

       this year, next year, sometime, never
       en roule-en ma boule roule-en
       we'll be friends for ever and ever

Pimperroquet, le roi des papillons
se faisant la barbe, il
se coupa le menton
une, une, c'est la lune
deux, deux, c'est le jeu
seven, eight   trois, trois – c'est a toi!
nine, a-laura
ten a-laura   echod, shtaim
Secord   hamelech bashomayim
echod, shtaim, sholosh, ar-ba . . .

whereja get the cold, sir?
up at the North Pole, sir;
what were ya doin there, sir?
catchin Polar bears, sir;
how may didja catch, sir?
one, sir; two sir
Salome was a dancer
she did the hootchykootch
she shook her shimmy shoulder
and showed a bit too much

my boyfriend's name is Fatty
he comes from Cincinnati

my boyfriend's name is Jello
he comes from Monticello

ini ini maini mo
que cheleque palesto
que jingale lestingo
ini ini maini mo

and this is the way you played
begin:

ordinary throw the ball against the fence, catch it
moving same thing, don't move your feet *laughing*
mustn't show your teeth *talking*
shut, your, mouth
                        one hand that's how you
catch it *the other hand*
one foot pick it up, you dope *the other foot*
and
clap front, clap back
                        *front&back, back&fron*t
tweedle with your hands like twiddling your thumbs
only overhand
twydle underhand *curtsey, salute*
and *roundabout*
                        catch it and
start from *moving*

over the whole thing without
stirring from the spot slap
your leg for *one foot* wave your
arms for *roundabout* on through *laughing* ononon

TILL YOU GET TO *BIG MOVING* !!!

particle, atom, molecule, world
solar system, galaxy, supergalaxy, cosmos

but start with small, the ball on the wall
that's how it went, and begin again:

> my boyfriend's name is Tonto
> he comes from New Toronto
> with twenty-four toes
> and a pickle on his nose
> and this is the way my story goes:

◆

we
started
something
like a slug
and grew without
a thought or wish to
something like a fish a
frog a bird a pig a golly-
wog and ultimately red and
born a blueblack head or
peppercorn or bald or
blind or idiot or
multiheaded
poly-
glot

◆

$I = I$
$I? = ?I$
$?W?H?Y?$
$?I = I?$

$I = not$
$ALL/eye/see$
$= (s/m)uch$
$= notme$

(rockabye baby the cradle is hard
yer pa got it outa the junkman's backyard)

the thing that I thought was the moon
turned out to be Mother's face
or Sister's or Brother's or Dad's or the cat's
—there's notme all over the place

(but I want the world's food in my belly
I want all the things I can see
I want all the toys in the world in my arms
and I want all the arms around ME)

black skin, drum belly
little stick leg
Papa paint the sores on
hold your hands and beg

◆

What shall we name the baby?
William? or James? or John?
Matthew? or Mark? or maybe
even Napoleon?

sticks and stones can break my bones
but names'll never hurt me
and when I'm dead and in my grave
you'll be sorry for what you called me

whatcher name?
Dickery Dame
ask me agin
and I'll tell ya the same . . .

. . . the secret power, the personal key
the three golden hairs in the forehead of the Giant
the stone in the yoke in the egg in the duck
in the rabbit in the basket in the chest beneath the Oak

in the Oak of the Golden Bough
in the magical Mistletoe:

'In the whole of the East Indian Archipelago
the etiquette is the same
no-one utters his own name . . .'

Sha-ame, sha-ame!
everybody knows yer na-ame!

Whatcher name?
Mary Jane
wheredya live?   comment t'appelle tu?
down a lane   je m'appelle comme mon pere
whatcher number?   et ton pere?
cucumber   mon pere s'appelle comme moi

it's Dinger Bell and Dusty Miller, Moishe Tochas
       and Lumber Bonce
it's *mwele* and Elkeh Pipick, Scaevola, Pepito and
       Tanglefoot . . .

what do they call' y'?
Patchy Dolly
where were y' born?
in the cow's horn

                    ◆

where were ya born? I didn't hear ya
roundabout and begin again
well I'll tell ya

my father was born in England
my mother was born in France
but I was born in diapers
because I had no pants

(cross my heart and hope to die
if I ever tell a lie)

where were you born my pretty lass?

born in the still-house bin
ifn Pappy hadn picked me outa the mash
they'd'a called me Stone Blind Gin

where do you come from, Cotton-Eye Joe?
way down south where the taters grow

where do you come from, Vinegar Bill?
where the Gila sleeps in the sagebrush hill

where do you come from, Popoli
in your *laplap* jockstrap sewn with bead?
I'm growing up in New Guin-ea
under the eye of Margaret Mead

laughing, talking, one hand, the other hand
one foot, the other foot
that's where the shoe is
roundabout

◆

how's your old man earn his nicker?
potter? piper? peapod-picker?
packer? knacker? sailor? stoker?
bumbailiff? or bailbond-broker?
doctor? proctor? thane? or thief?
dustman? postman? on relief?

my old man's a dustman
he wears a dustman's hat—

aah, knock it off, Noddy
we already been there

my old man's a navvy
a navvy by his trade
he wheels a great big barrow
he swings a pick and spade

my old man's a navvy
he get's a navvy's pay
it doesn't fill a rotten tooth
or scare the wolf away

I'm growin up to earn my keep
as quickly as I can
an I guess I'll be a navvy
just like my old man

my father works in the A&P
my mother clerks in the baker-y
my sister dances in the hula show
and they do it for me, me, me

my old man's a psychiatrist
he has a psychiatrist's couch
he doesn't stick any needles in
but his patients still cry *ouch*!

he thinks I'm slightly paranoid
or maybe rather manic
I tell him I'll turn out all right
if only he won't panic

if you got anxiety
my dad will worry for you
at 25 bucks an hour
it's what psychiatrists do

◆

Why?—Z
butter your bread
if you don't like it
go to bed

Why? Why? Why?
¿Cuándo? Pourquoi? Far vus?

why does a chicken cross the road?
no hablo español

waarom steekt een kip weg over?
pourquoi non?

¿cuándo la gallina cruza la carretera?
vais ich?

perchè Garibaldi alla battaglia di Calatafimi
        portava le bretelle tricolori?
to hold his pants up, stupid

◆

how and when and where and why
stars and sun and moon and sky

canals and craters, dunghills, dunes
tell me what's beyond the moons?

beyond the moons the sands are deep
they spread through all the purple skies
in them are Giants who never sleep
but watch the world with burning eyes

they're just like us, with sharper claws
huger pincers, fiercer jaws
and if they catch you—goodbye head!
goodbye little crystal bed!

so wrap your feelers round your feet
fold your thorax nice and neat
the sun is high, the hour is late
now it's time to estivate

    I lay me in my quartzy pool
    I pray the gods to keep it cool
    to keep off demons far and near
    and wake me when the winter's here
    to dance with joy on all my legs
    and live to lay a thousand eggs

           ◆

    Mother Mother I am sick
    call for the doctor quick quick quick!!!
    Doctor Doctor shall I die?

    Yes my child and so I shall I . . .

Do you ever think when the hearse goes by
that one of these days you're going to die?
a-whoo, a-whoo . . .

the dark the hairy scary dark's where
the nightblooming neuroses grow:

Mummy the THING'S under my bed again!

they wrap you up in a big white shirt
and cover you over with tons of dirt
a-whoo . . .

under my bed, my childhood bed
only the dustflocks blew
in the midnight caverns of my head
the goblins spawned and grew

they stuff you into a long long box
and cover you over with mountains of rocks
a-whoo . . .

but my children's fears are wider, wilder
fiercer, freer
in their delirious feverdreams
angry shadows chatter from the bookshelves
and Caesar's legions fight all Gaul from the staircase
landing
        imperial ibises rise
stark and threatening from the reeds of the rug

and the worms crawl out and the worms crawl in
and the ones that crawl in are lean and thin
and the ones that crawl out are fat and stout
a-whoo, a-whoo . . .

deposition by J.E.G., acquaintance of writer:

The storm was raging and the wind was howling out-
side the castle. Inside the castle the lights flickered of.
There was a blood-curling shriek. A Black figure stalked
up the corridor. Bloodstained was his hands. I ran down
the corridor and fell. Quickly I got up. I ran down the
corridor only to find a girl jabbed in the back. As I ran
farther I fell in a pit. It was a donjon! I felt myself being
chained to the wall. I struggled to free myself only to get
whipped in the leg. The lights went on, I found the
Black thing ready to cut my throat! I prepared to die. I'M
DEAD! I'M DEAD! I screamed.

your eyes fall in and your hair falls out
and your brains come tumb-a-ling down your snout
a-whoo . . .

Hap-py Birthday!
Hap-py Birthday!
children are crying
people are dying
Happy Birthday . . .

here you're in
there you're out
that's how the world goes
roundabout!

◆

rise, Sally, rise
open your eyes
the earth turns east, the sun turns west
turn to the one you love best

Red Rover, Red Rover, let Billy come over
I wish, I wish your wish may come true
the sun is up high at the top of the sky
you can't cross my river unless you wear blue

bushel of wheat, bushel of barley
all not hid, holler Charley!
bushel of wheat, bushel of rye
all not hid, holler I!
bushel of wheat, bushel of clover
all not hid can't hide over

look out, World! here I come!

we sing from near, we sing from far
you brought us here, and here we are

we sing from far, we sing from near
nobody told us why we're here

we sing by night, we sing by day
nobody told us what to say

in love begot, in lust begot
nobody asked us what we thought

◆

my warriors have pitched their tents
where Tigris meets Euphrates
I suck the stubborn teats of goats
and feed upon the date-trees

I hunker down upon my heels
(they call me chieftain's daughter)

and I crack my lice between my nails
and flick them in the water

    we have to sing, we sing a song
    it's all of Time and twice as long

         ◆

    Black sheep, black sheep, have you any wool?

    Yes, Master Coxe, my fleece is fat and full

    Shearer, shearer, clip him to the fell
    and take the wool to little John who lives by the well

I sit and pick at wool
I pick at wool all day
I have no time to go to school
I have no time to play

the shepherds tend the flocks
the shearers clip their backs
and sell the wool to Thomas Coxe
who stuffs it into sacks

and when the bags are full
they bring them in to me
for every day I pick the wool
he pays my penny fee

my hands are cracked and sore
I pray to go to heaven
and hope perhaps he'll pay me more
next year when I am seven

I sing my song the whole day long
from morning light to even

◆

I am a little chimney sweep
a poor benighted chap
I knock about the dark all day
and no-one cares a rap

the soot grinds down into my groins
each time my brush goes whap!
I'll die from cancer of the nuts
if I don't get the clap

we sing our song, our song is long
it's large as life and twice as strong

if you should see a chimney sweep
your luck will turn to bad
so always keep your eyes away
from a chimney-sweeping lad

but if by chance they light on one
don't let it go at that
—just hold your collar till you see
a horse, a dog, a cat . . .

◆

here upon the altar
lies the bleeding victim
we slew him without falter
—that was why we picked him

O mighty Rongo, here's your fish
wrapped up in tidy parcels

was ever god served up a dish
of such prodigious morsels?

all the gods are bad ones
and some are worse than others
the god who gave me his name
had demons for his brothers

he chose the altar for me
the axe to split my head
the leaves to wrap my ears and nose
for the prize when I was dead

the missionary came then
and he took me in his arm
he swore *his* God would strike them dead
if they did me any harm

my father broke his spear in two
the prayer-king stove his drum
and as a joyful Christian child
I sing of Kingdom Come!

◆

one day he gave me peaches
one day he gave me pears
one day he gave me fifty cents
to kiss him on the stairs

the missionary ladies
have taught me to sew and cook
to plant flowers in pots
and embroider French knots
and write in a bluelined book

they have taught me to read the Bible
and to frown and turn my back
on Corporal McGlash
when he twirls his moustache
and calls me the Rose of Ladakh

but my mother will come and fetch me
to my home on the mountain side
and I'll turn back my face
to the ways of my race
in Shamlegh when I am a bride

and turquoise and silver will bind up my hair
instead of a flowery hat
my three husbands will plough
while the fourth milks the cow
—but I won't tell the pastor that.

    I gave him back his peaches
    I gave him back his pears
    I only kept the fifty cents
    and kicked him down the stairs

◆

Mammy, Mammy, tell me true
when shall we be free?

Hush, chile, eat you chickenfoot stew
don't say dem things to me
    ole Uncle Jack he wanta git free
    foun his way north by de bark on de tree
    cross dat river floatin in a tub
    paterollers gibm a mighty close rub

Mammy, Mammy, all de years
Massa laid us low

Hush, chile, hush chile, all you tears
won' make him let us go
    old Aunt Dinah jes like me
    wuk so hard she wanta git free
    but Aunt Dinah gittin kinda ole
    she feared of Canada cause it so cole

Mammy, wanta board dat Freedom Train
feel de sun shine on my haid

Hush, chile! don't talk out so plain
or you mighty close to dead!
    ole Uncle Billy, mighty fine man
    tote de news to Massa, fast as he can
    tell Uncle Billy you want free fer a fac
    nex day de hide skun offn you back

and still we dance and still we sing
Juba dancers in a ring!

Juba dis an Juba dat
Juba skin dat Yaller Cat

Juba jump and Juba sing
Juba cut dat Pigeon's Wing!

Gadder roun, chillun, thank de Lawd
old Abe done set us free
Massa in de cole cole groun, praise Gawd
in de Year of Jubilee!

Missus an Massa, walkin down street
hans in dere pockets, nothin to eat
Missus git home, wash up de dishes!
patch up y'ole man's raggedy britches!

Massa run home, git out de hoe
clear de weeds outa y'own corn row
de Kingdom Come, de slaves gone free
ain no slaves in de Year Jubilee!

two four six eight
we don't want to integrate

> (*'I dunno what they complainin about what with
> Bull Connor givin em free street
> baths an dog shows ever day'*)

put down you heel
put down you toe
    ever time you turn aroun
    you stomp Jim Crow!

git off you knees
hold up you head
    ever time you turn aroun
    Jim Crow dead!

◆

get a piece of pork and
stick it on a fork and
shove it in the mouth of a Jewboy, Jew . . .

a skinny kid, a Yidl kid, I run the streets of Kiev
the sh'gutzim kick my shins, the cold winds blow me like a leaf
a skinny kid, a Yidl kid, with swinging black earlocks
for furtrimmed ladies and their gents my father fixes clocks
he cheats them just a little bit to make up for the tax
I call them *Pan* and *Panya* and I spit behind their backs
a dirty sheeny ragged Yid I spit behind their backs

    Jewboy, Jew
    Jewboy, Jew

I am Belsen number 7829
I know not blue sky nor to see the sun shine
blind, I hear others die. I am called swine.

    and still we sing and still we sing
    and through the wires our voices ring

does no-one hear? does no-one come?
Lord of the World, my mouth is dumb

    ◆

    Bach Jones a bag of bones
    a belly full of fat
    and when he dies he shuts his eyes
    now what do you think of that?

at Aberfan where I began
I never grew to be a man
the slag ran down toward the town
I cried and I was still
God lost my name and no-one came
I died beneath the hill

still in their dreams our voices sing
through stone and slime the echoes ring

> Rhys Owen was a holy man
> he went to church on Sunday
> to pray to God to give him strength
> to whip the boys on Monday!

◆

the light swings west, the shadows follow
the ball is hollow
on the wall

curtsey, salute and roundabout
we go by turns but never out

we turn the world away from night
we raise the sun, we bring the light

if we don't act the way we should
too bad for you. We're here for good.

and begin again

Shadow Is a Man

what is man that God shall regard him
what is man that time shall reward him
death retard him?

shadow is a man
is a shadow man

what is God that man shall regard Him
what is God that prayer shall reward Him
shall o-lord Him?

shadow man like a god
hides his face behind his hand
burns his tree

bloods his sand

what is man and the son of man?

shadow is a man
with his rod divides the sea
and his sperms multiply
the aspects of the sky

pits his head against the womb
plants his fingers in the death
sucks at dust and wonders why
he has no breath

what is man O Lord
what is man that Death must devise him
where the angel man must refuse him
stop his trumpet
break his wings
blind his eyes
where is man that man recognize him?

shadow man

Jennie Gotlieb Bardikoff

cashed in her chips
& oh how she loved them   we found
forty decks of clubs spades hearts & diamonds
after she left

did you play cards last night? I asked
nothing, shpielt a rummy

her body a battleground for surgical bayonets
tubes catheters monitors shunts i.v. and shots
all she wanted was a good cup of coffee

and when they dragged her round the bed like a rag doll
nothing moving in her but pain
she said *it's enough*

told the shivering children their faces were flowers
whispered then she liked the daughter-in-law
more than a little
and was home free

she never did care for whiskey
said a whiff of the stuff put her out   I suppose
because she had so much firewater
pumping her heart already

Song

o children are the snow
their crystal
growth mysterious
the compass of a grain of dust
its tempered star

children if I could find you find you
in those deltas of sea and sand
that land the snow
has drifted down upon

but they are crystalline
cry *touchmenot touchmenot! I*
melt on your hand!

children
am I the sun?

Down in Black and White

in the danish sex manual
(written in lyrical french)
a naked couple arrange themselves
modestly body covering groin faces
turned away or curtained
with their wisp dark hair, they are
dark ectomorphs and seem unscandinavian

yet they are legible: she sunbathes
in bikini pants on holidays, has chapped elbows
and stub nails, works in a dull job
perhaps a waitress, slouches around home in
loose buttoned sweaters;
                              he has sore heels
a student in ill-fitting shoes, the line of his neck
and shoulder are familiar on the street
their soles are black from the splintered studio
floor
      they are young, graceful, vulnerable: foretaste
the *lotus* and the *tree* for slender lovers
of yoga.
         they are cool toward each other.
she does not serve him his fried potatoes. she
is from another part of town and he has
affairs of his own. they never meet.

Hip Hip

in that year in Crystal Beach
the mayflies blew
blue blew   in that year
their drifted ghosts
host of heaven blowing wide
                            I
never saw them fly only
white winged carapaces blew
on my face   in my hair
and I never saw them grow
in those jettisoned shellsockets only
blowing in the street
washing corners in the wind
translucent and undead
                            I
never saw them fly alive
only dust against the feet
without the crisp of breaking
or the whisper of a wind
in that year
in Crystal Beach   when they blew

Roll the Bones

the subway passes the grave stones
and the bones turn over
the quick red car groans
into the cave and the bones turn over
passes the Mutual Security
the Bible Society
the Pie In The Sky Corp
oration
      the faces
in the subway car are
half-forgotten half-seen-before
never saw them before in my life
say the tracks and wheels   and
the bones turn over

Home on the Ward

the men at the pool table in rolled sleeves
are tough and muscular
                              even the gut
one of them has looping over his belt
looks hard
                where's Jack?
upstairs
          stubs on their lips
flicker smoke

indifferent players, their game is
swinging their backsides and cue butts
round the corner pockets
in wild shots grinning piratically
to scatter the benched visitors

small wiry nurses give them the go-by
he jumpy?
              yeah   he don't feel like comin down
you want another?

                    chalk the cues
dribble smoke, sinewy arms
bandaged over the slashes
                              thin skin
bruises easy and scars hard
and the shadows fight back
they will take their pills

In the Noonday

Two black men with blind white canes
crouch in the hot brick shadow, one
sits on a crate, elbowing knees, reflexive
gaze at the blank sun on the bland
uncoloured cornea, face twisted
toward the street, straining
for the immaterial world to meet him
face on.
          The other, by the wall,
probes the pits of his eyes with
fingers, reaching sensory tips for the electric
nerve ends of his sockets;
face covered, his hands will serve, they say
in midnight blacker than his skin, all colours one
except love. Their canes lie
every which way across the sidewalk waiting
to trip you, and the men
having no other recourse than
arrogance asks compassion.

On the Beach

tonight the sailors are walking in twos like nuns
hands rise in tandem to breast pockets for passes as
police accost them: there are three kinds
lined up here waiting for trouble
Long Beach local, Shore Patrol, Military. there is no
trouble. the summerwhite
sailors are a little subdued, like nuns.

the girls and I play skeeball, trying for rich prizes
win a ring with an anonymous green stone for our
lump of dogeared score tickets; Max
shoots pool with my son; his French wife
pale as the evening cloud and quieter
sits on a bench knitting
dollclothes for my daughter; her
diamonds flash
                    puddles flicker
with the lights of the midway
                                    carousels mutter jerkily
turning in sleep. I don't want to know
how the scrawny caged cock will pick out YANKEE DOODLE
on some kind of string thing if I put a dime in the slot

Max
watches girls: they stack, size shape and colour
like bottles on shelves behind a bar (he has tended bar)
his blue eyes gleam and his marvellous curly mouth
quirks in delight: *Isn't it good, hah?* popcorn cartons
roll down the alleys on damp night windstreams *ain't
you glad I brought you?*

walking back to the Lincoln we say *Sure, Max
no question about it. absolutely.*

The Usual

when I talk of love
if it makes your teeth ache
sorry   it does not *pleure dans mon coeur*
comme il pleut sur la ville
I drag my nails down my scabbed heart
till it's ridged as an Ashanti warrior's face
and forbidding

say it is a ship
registered under the Liberian flag
riding its bilge, old rust & shifting oil
it beats, it beats

you've heard everything beats like a heart
birds' wings or engines, everyone
takes the world's pulse
tell me what a heart beats like then?
in fire a star

I know whose heart
attends a strange measuring device
a marvel of chronologic accuracy
I set my clocks by, it is my pacemaker
beats a yard apart, a fathom deep
through its chest wall I swear I hear it say
timeless, timeless

my old scarred lug's a
blood veteran, stormbringer
inharmonious organ fitted with
pipes, bellows, wheezes, lubdubb and oh
my workaday love, my love
my Monday love

Premises

if I were Earth and you were Earthshaker
if I were the sea and you a well-keeled ship
if I were the Tree of Life and you the life in it

I'd open the bark and come, a greensap river
to flow in your live space between earth and sky
rise up in a whirlwind, for women
are given the names of cyclones
cleave at a touch beyond
bedrock, into the magma

for my living green you would invent new forms and motions
stand safe in the eye of my circle of breath and marvel
and from the raw fire you'd build mountains

Seeing Eye

Stop dreaming said Sevenix
"I must dream" said Mercator "Last night"
I was reading about places where there are
        trees & sky, earth & air, sweat & snot
velvet & burlap, dust & dung
markets and ships sailing and mountains and men
    in rags"
            I know, I read them with you said Sevenix
"and I want to see them all"
            You will never
"I know and it doesn't matter" said Mercator

Why are you looking in the mirror? Dalud asked
"Because you never see me, you only see what I
see, I could be faceless for all you know, the way
    you make use of me
                    what would you see if I made
    love to you, Klavvia? only yourself"
Close your eyes then said Klavvia *I will know your*
face with my hands and all your other places
        "When I close my eyes you go blind, all
        of you, but now
    you can all see me for a change when I
        look in the mirror" said Mercator

"I have green eyes with black centres
                            yours are the
colour of steel, pupil-less and they shine like steel
        their sockets are full of the nerve-
fibres that suck the images from my brain and
    I hate you for making me what I
        am" said Mercator

"what will you be when I'm dead?"
Both blind and mad said Sevenix
in the bursting panic of the ultimate dark
"Then you must learn to handle the ship's controls"
Mercator said
We know now, but who will read
the gauges for us, Mercator?

"I don't know or care, I'm going up front
to look for comfort in the Book:
Log of the Colony Ship Pharos IV the drifting ship
that forgot where it's going if it ever knew
hundreds of years back
find balm in the old story
of explosion, trembling voices on tapereels
broken machines, anguished scribblings with a pen
radiation burns and death, years of repairs and later
dear God, strange mutations, horrified cliché
telepathy and blindness in one package: miraculous
gift of the Magi" said Mercator

"dominance and genetic drift, and I
am the last of your Seers, your eyes not for sea and earth
but for white fires black sky and gauges"
Mercator
"and everything depends on me, oh I know
you need me and when I die you go mad and"
Mercator, we
"even if I had a child it would be blind, a
blind thinker, so
don't come touching me, Klavvia, stay back"
We love you, Mercator
"I know, oh how I know. You love me. I
want to be dead, I am nothing, I am
your dog" said Mercator

Cosmology

when we sailed to the edge of the universe
in our cockleshell, our coracle
they gave us speeches and good wishes
theories they couldn't explain the nature of
we had our suspicions

I don't know why we all dressed in black
hardly ever spoke
made love to the music of the *Symphonie Fantastique*
Judith played with her hair, braided, braided her hair
and the synapses exploded everywhere

Yorick rattled knucklebones and blew his pennywhistle
Bar Hillel sang of a drowning skull
Jean Baptiste preached of the end of days
as we swam the circumference of the darkness
sailed the days, in the days, end of days

till we stopped stuck fast in the midden of a void
where the parabolic comets dropped
beyond the planets' hoops, and someone cried

      FIAT LUX!
      LET THERE BE LIGHT!
      VE YEHI OR!

nothing answered but the pounding on the door
the pulsing vein outside the door

we crept out of the shell
and felt along the wall
beneath the filament, the firmament, the
membrane

      bone we said and nodded
      every head its gut-strung puppet
      and stood still

and stood still
in the crater of the skull
in the ossuary place in the limit of the cosmos
where we'd come with a wish
and a whistle and suspicion

to the ending of the song, at the limit of the word
on the edge of cognition, of creation

Scratch

there is no history.
civilization never began.
I make the first mark always:
here woman, there man.
every day the sky lightens
I defy you. I deny
contradiction. it is as I say.
there is no history. I mark it
learning the first time.
scratch and start again.
as long as bones are disjointed
in desert places. scratch.
You rebuke my works
how long, Lord? if not now when?
flies suck lips, birds pick eyes
in the blasted acres.
scratch. Lord, begin again.

Cenacle

ah Lord, what's that bunch up to now?
Simon says it's the last time he'll have them in the house
Simon says abc one day and xyz the next
only thirteen he says, thirteen
not counting the women, them
pecking their noses in my pots, rolling matzot
in my kitchen, soldiers
slamming shields on the door
yelling for food I hadn't got, servant girl
running out to the well and caught there
coming with torn skirts and swollen eyes
mouth twisted she won't tell, oh
I can tell you, soldiers
feed these thirteen, says Simon
where was I to get money for meat, Lord, meat?
not looking at me Simon says
pock nose stubbed leper hands
feed them
Lord, I sold my carcass to the butcher for their meat
thick bloody fingers ripping the flanks in two
into my flesh
ripe tastes better, he tells me, nails sharp as his knives
I know where blood flows
thirteen
hangdog the lot of them on the way to a bad end
in my upper room, never raised eyes to me
serve them
this their festival? one says
I will be betrayed   what wonder? flesh
Lord, sacrificed for the meat
that one I felt bad for, had it in his face
and the other worse, with the eyes: *I will betray*
the one: *my body, my blood the bread and wine*
and the rest cried for him
                              I don't begrudge weeping
and I know trapping
but that sick-eyed one, alone, my Lord, I know
the body and blood

ms & mr frankenstein

        Scarpino and I had this thing
going upstairs in a downtown house
    he dismantled the skylight first I
mean a thing with an old wroughtiron fence he got
            from a contractor for the armature
                commission he said
                that's what he said
    built up past the TV antenna   landlord
        picking up Pittsburgh yelling *Get that thing down!*
NEXT WEEK says Scarpino don't ask how welding
        letting fly
            rust jets and paint curlicues
    into a black stick man NOW
says Scarpino EPOXY MASKING TAPE and ARTIFACTS
MAN OF THE CENTURY!!! MADE ON THE PREMISES!!!   gluing
    cuphandles dented percolator baskets
            potlids nonreturnable bottles
    twisted tinties coffeemill-wheels
            cracked dollsheads rundown alarmclocks
paperclips shoelaces nailpolish-brushes
        typewriter keys
                    that made 1/2 a leg
 and the night I spent hacking him out of the epoxy
gave the thing most of a pair of overalls & a jockstrap
    we still had
                lampshades windowblinds
    cornpoppers shishkebab-skewers knifesharpeners
    bent forks axehandles beercans shavingcream containers

    Scarpino wild with welding gluing winding
    till we got what looked like 2/3 of
        Ozymandias King of Kings
and I begged, Scarpino, don't you think enough — and he
    BELOVED gave me an abstract kiss could have
        got more juice out of a Rodin marble DARLING
        WE MUST SCROUNGE AND SCAVENGE
            he always talked like that

IT IS ART DEAREST HEART!!
if it had been January he could have gone to hell

but what with night youth and the May moon
I mined the dumps for paintscrapers andirons winecorks
tin funnels paperweights runningshoes raingauges
dull hacksaws sprung springs bicyclespokes tenpenny nails
gum erasers toothpaste-tubes broken staplers spent matches
plugged nickels
he welded wild and mad
arm & thigh of his mighty man
& I was getting a little off on the thing myself maybe
the glue
some weird trip good God
how we'd get it out of there
or where

it grew
smashed headlights ashtrays burnt bulbs
popcan-rings empty ballpoints cereal-boxes
crochet-hooks pacifiers cigarette-holders
last year's calendars candle-stubs speedometers
tongue-depressors dipsticks
lipsticks ticket-stubs ladles with handles
strawberry-hullers china dogs
I'm out of breath
& flat on the floor by the time Scarpino says
DONE!!!

there stands Man Matterhorn
by Easter Island out of Las Vegas
& a soup song of King Kong

COLOSSAL breathed Scarpino and fell to his knees
well its head was up there in the stars
25 foot high and every inch a junkman

so being a bit woozy with this bottle of Old Bubble
    not having magic names or electric jolts
      and it didn't have much of a noble brow or prow
    still I felt it needed a little ceremony you understand
up there on the scaffold Scarpino dancing around singing
    THERE'LL BE A HOT TIME IN THE OLD TOWN TONIGHT
    climbed up dizzy don't ask
    & bashed Godzilla's eyeless head with old Bubble

    and he gave some kind of shiver
    and his mouth opened

honest I wasn't all that scared
just thought he'd say something friendly like
hello there honey   but he jerked
and squeaked
        that was the wroughtiron innards
and blinked
and ticked and whirred and whirled and went
ma-ma ma-ma
and sparked buzzed clanked cracked flashed foamed
twanged squirted spilled snapped tapped
stapled snipped crackled crocheted
sharpened sawed slurped threaded popped
hulled honked scraped crunched zinged

    scaffold shaking like oyoy old Scarp down there
      doing Yoga exercises singing
      GOT IT ALL TOGETHER YEAH, YEAH
that mindless mouth *wa wa wa*
        I wanted out
slid down the shook frame
  chachachattering and whooee
    a kind of cloudy glory
      gathered from the sky
and Thing just raised his arms twitching forty ways
    and cleared his throat and cried out

COSMOS I COME!

zapped out the roof on a pillar of fire
blowing a hole clear down the cellar
knocking the landlord out taking along
Scarp's wig & false teeth my fillings
& the bandaid from my thumb where I'd
cut it on the damn thing
                              neighbours yelling
Lightning, by Gawd!
                 we ducked out before the landlord came to
also slipped the cops the Fire Dept & the Board of Health

        sleeping in weedy lots under newspapers
about *RCMP Probes Bomb Plot   New Comet Sighted*   Scarpino
half off his nut for days raving

HE IS OUR EMISSARY TO THE UNIVERSE!!!!

he she it shit I wonder
just what kind of garbage they're gonna be sending us

        anyway old Scarp got over it looking pretty thin
without the rug & choppers and my teeth hurt
        so we split he went up to learn
            bone carving from the Inuit
and I moved in with a plumber and that's the story

Was/Man

whenever the moon went into eclipse he became a man
lost quite a lot of hair, his fangs pulled in about half an inch
and he put on heavy muscle in shoulder, buttock and thigh
he wasn't bothered losing the tail and claws so much, it was
growing the crazy complex inefficient
nose vexed him. sometimes the transformation
caught him in the middle of a howl & he sneezed
his eyes stayed harsh and feral. the moon darkened
he picked up on it quickly enough, bathed in the windblown
rainpool, shaved, kicked the year's collection of
bones out of the closet looking for the roll-on
shook the moths from the woollens, shoved his feet
clumsily in the shoes, dragged on an old
trenchcoat & a fedora and caught the fast freight

town wasn't much, a few bright lights in the plaza
and the all-nitery. people in that place
were rather morose and surly, but it
suited him down to the ground.
                                        he enjoyed
a few cigarillos, and whiskey in moderation
girls who didn't mind the hairy type liked him. he never
bit them, just grizzled a little.
                                        at first he found all that
grown flesh of his luxurious, new senses nipping him
every minute, but when the moon's scythe edged out
he wanted to gnaw on himself, drag off the excrescence
caught himself thinking of barred places, jail, cage, zoo
got scared he'd be trapped in his strange meat, man till he died.
found he wanted to pick fights with dark grumbling
figures in the eye-stinging smoke. he lit out for home
under the quarter-moon.

not snapping back in 2 flicks like some movie monster
he knew he'd be at it again, folded & packed the trappings neatly
but his wild thighs tightened, went to the sweet ground
the claws sprung,

he dug his beloved snout into the scents
of wood-rot and wet leaves, sharpened the fangs
lengthening from the roof and floor of his jaws, he had
an hour or two of the moonlit night to run in
though his eyes were redrimmed from the smoke
of the bar and poolroom
                              and he
dashed water in his thickening fur to douse the rank
civil insidious urge of the secret man

The Rest of History

old Adam, old Eve
make love in a calm bed

Cain, Abel
raise crook and hoe
stoptime in bloodied air, the red
earth drinks then

there are Seth, Enos, and
others to make multitudes

old Adam, old Eve
light candles and bless bread

old Adam, old Eve
dream in a green bed

The Robot's Daughter

I wanted to grow
a hot heartbeating centre
a flickering cloud of brain

instead I grew
hook lens antenna
a ticking meter
a coil of spring

Mother!

what song have I to sing?

Red Black White

blood ink paper have been my life I bore
children in a slush of blood
dreamed in a scratch of ink
and that damned white paper
with words to be written everywhere

Pneumonia Dreams 105°

I

Nothingness wrapped in
crumbled earth and dead leaves

II

I am fitting a map of the Outer Hebrides
over a man's left shoulder

III

I have bought a two-dollar
lottery ticket in France
and the Canadian government wants me
to fill out 6 big cartons of tax forms
written in the style of Milton's *Areopagitica*

IV

my wonderful new computer font
has letters that jump up and
dance when I look at them

V

the space liner in geosynchronous
orbit over Newfoundland is a brilliant sunlight-
white cluster of new and ancient ships and stations
travelling for twenty-five hundred years, it has
five thousand to go
                I hear voices calling
to and from: *don't forget me, I love you,*
give my love
           the alien contingent
half shark, half polar bear, wants me
to find the musical note that will help them
defeat their enemies

VI

I am writing this poem

What I Know (Making Free With Villon's *Smalltalk*)

I know how to ring down a chime of dimes
in a dime slot if you can find me a dime slot,
I know how to push the button at a stoplight
so the red flicks green before you blink, and
I know how to do a cat's cradle behind my back;
I know how to love a stem and a leaf
so the flower reaches up to kiss me
but other than that, I don't know anything

and I am the greatest of puzzle solvers:
give me two letters of a 14-letter word you got it,
and words, I know every word spoken in jest
and every lying word because every
lie is as weak as a cobweb, because
everyone who believes a lie is a liar
to the own self, oh sure, I know all that
but other than that I'm an ignoramus.

I know where there is love deep as a river
and I know how to swim in it, thank God,
and also the bitterness of the seas it can decant into,
but the thready fibrillations of its sources are mysteries
to me, and though I know how to love a soul alive
I'm damned if I know how to make a soul rejoice.
I give up on it. I don't know anything.

O François, I know how to rip off one of your ballades
and add a little archy to make it my own
and I know how to end a line with a whipcrack,
but other than that I don't know anything.

One More Riff On Villon's
Helmet-Maker's Woman

I thought I heard the old woman raging in the street
about how her beauty had vanished like last years' snow:

"It has melted from my bones and I am only the shadow
of a radiance that drew kings from the weight of their crowns—"

She was howling up a storm and thumping her breast
bared to the weather and the years that wrinkled it—

"Lightning and thunder smash me and be damned to you!
you can't beat at me any more than age does!"

Dragging her sordid life of knotted sacks in a rusted market wagon
she wraps a babushka round her withered neck and the trailings
of her hair are owned by the wind:
                        "O life! this body a beggar
would sneer at, all gone that was loved by ministers of state
smooth forehead, mouth like an open rose
and thighward a gate with a rose
garden in it, that too many men had the key of
crumpled, and hands red leaves of November that were white
and narrow as virgins, all gone into sooted snows
melted into gutteral
drains, and all of an old year's snows . . ."

The Lover

so what became of that helmet-maker
home from the wars, whose woman
howled up the streets and
down the alleys, her beauty stolen by life?

may be a scarred and shrunk-up fellow squinting by a
thin fire with some bit of dead meat spitted on it,
his tongs and hammers rusted

far away are they that must have been
biting each other's hearts out
then all ends well for that

Mother

I

My mother's in the album, on the wall, in dream
a little surly curly in a plaid dress
leaning on Papa and Mama in a pout

Papa deserted the Czar's army
ran till he reached Canada
He only stayed long enough
to have his picture taken
she said, and there he's framed above her
in dark cloth and gold stars
leaning on a pillar

II

Now here she's flanked by Mama and baby sisters
beadblack eyes and mouth a pursed frightened line
sweet natural joyfulness already blunted
gingersnap's cynic wit fast muffled
by obscure terrors

Papa dead young of influenza, no money
for design school, prisoner of
Grandma's drygoods store
sewing on dolls' clothes forever more

III

until my father rescued her
in his swagging great Grey Dort
(sweet loving fellow)
the Grey Dort stalled but all was mellow
for one brave moment
(sweet hapless fellow
of springsteel honesty)

IV

and there again, her sharp child's face
weighed by the fruity hat, she sinks
drowning in the fur coat her father-in-law made
for some six-footer

producing the one child, thought it was a doll,
made it into a doll, was filled with terror
that it might not be a doll

yet on the sidewalk
there, in front of the Tuscarora Apts.,
in sunny 1927
kneeling on one knee she holds me,
mouth in a smiling O

V

Trapped by the family business and frail-hearted
my father sheltered her, himself
prisoner of all those movie houses
ancestral picture palaces
east west & north, the city's limits

hectored by Uncle Max
'cause I'm your boss! I'll be your boss
forever!
his boss forever

VI

and then still young her Prince of Everything
died, and everything was nothing

His death cut out her heart. The amputation
cut off her body. 35 years she lived
in that same house
in that same pain
with the same wooden leg
that creaked in winter
mowing the summer lawn and savouring
when neighbours asked
Why doesn't Phyllis do that for you
Mary? (that nogoodnik girl)

VII

There were still pictures of
descendants wrinkling while grandchildren sprang
and there was the wheelchair
You'll always be my baby,
gripping my hands
I'm frightened! I'm afraid!

she died when I was on the ocean
faraway still
It was a dream, she said of life
a dream . . .

VIII

My mother never hovered in a dream of me
flew straight up to the sky
into the dream of a green tree
that was my father, where his
arm boughs sheltered her

the dream she came in was my daughter's
(how dare you have my dream!)
in her wheelchair crying
Nobody will remember me!
Dream-tough, dream-aunt Moxy said
Don't worry. Nobody will forget you.

IX

the wooden leg, stuff of my nightmares
went to the trash
with shoe and stocking on
pointed to the sky like Icarus'
foot out of the sea in Brueghel

X

I see her features rising up in me
now, the little tightness of the
mouth, with its quirked
muscles, and the sharp eye
as if they have been waiting
ever so long to be repeated here
in my mirror
and there on the sidewalk
(just by the mirror, from the oval frame)
still she presents me, still she cries O
surprised

XI

The day she died I first touched
paper with this poem
65 years I have been writing it

now bearing it like a shovel of hot coals
I offer it

Her Life

what I got left with after
the Chevra Kaddisha had
cleansed her body was a
thin gold ring and the
cheap watch I'd bought her
that she'd worn like a Cartier

I'd already sorted the
leaves of her life into a couple
of cardboard boxes, and years long
said goodbye to the clear
corridors of her mind

what I got left with was
like a light drift of ash
the thin breath of her
in an envelope that said:

one Timex watch
and
one gold wedding band

Thirty-Six Ways of Looking
at Toronto Ontario

1

the stacked plane circles, I
see my house, its angled street,
east, north, west, south,
southeast, northwest, there are
no parking places
here

2

we came in those years on the overnight train
from New York City along endless
lines of shimmering poplars
pounding on doors six am Customs yelling
Quite all right, we've seen naked people before!

3

poplar and all the
noble trees, oak, maple,
Maytime's chestnut in its candles
gingko, elm and ash
stand in their shade lace at
the height of June

4

on the white winter
streets, fir-trimmed, display their
wrought-iron armatures
naked they are so thick you cannot
see through them the
towers of pleated gold and seagreen glass
only the CN Tower (a latecomer) rises
cloudward & the Bank of Commerce
(tallest building in the British Empire, 1931)
stands humbled

5

the park here is a treeless square, worn lawn
furnished with the bust of
Sibelius in black granite
the wind sings his song

6

in shady Roselawn Cemetery
whether the wind is harsh or gentle
Uncle Max lies
among his three wives
Bébé, Didi and Claudette

7

at Queen's Park in long gone days & mine
a crocodile of children trail
their teacher to watch Mitch Hepburn
bald spot & waving arms
harangue his Legislature

8

the polar bear in Riverdale Zoo
roars in his narrow pool, his fur
stained yellow from city
smoke and filthy water

9

on Front Street the White Rose Gasoline
sign of ten thousand bulbs
blooms in a white bud
flares into petals and green leaves
fades and grows again

10

from the front lawn at
52 Kingston Rd in 1932
I watch the sun go down
over the wall of Woodbine Racetrack
trailing firelined clouds
and feel the glory of the ineffable
—real or a dream?

11

in the sunshine up Broadview Avenue
eight years old and happily-hoppiting
around the ancient stout cane-tottering
lady crowned in a Queen Mary hat
thinking (this is God's truth) I bet she wishes
she was a carefree little child like me

12

Sunday mornings north side of Queen has
an Edward Hopper light but upstairs
over the furrier shop my grandfather's
Yiddish tells my father's English the story
of the farmer and Czar I read
last week in Aesop about the
fisherman and the Emperor

13

writing senior fourth exams
(it's eighth grade now) three months
before that War with boys who'll die in it:
the summer window's open
there is a world out there, and it cries:
strawberry ripe!
strawberry ripe!

14

in Riverdale park where flashers slunk
and bobsleds ran longside the Dirty Don
now rivers of cars run with clean
bright-eye lights. I look crossyears
off Broadview to 9 Tennis Cres
where B15's lamplit. Hello, Child!

15

      3 SNAPS:

a young black man bare-chested in boxer
shorts dances down the street shadow-
boxing while his dog yips around him

16

two black men dandling a
gurgling blond baby
laugh and talk on a park bench

17

a deaf-mute
talking to himself
in sign language

18

      4 MOMENTS:

when I got home I found her in bed
with 2 other guys,
the cabbie says
I just stood there watching them, I couldn't
believe it

19

on the boardwalk the tall Texan in his Stetson
falls into step with us, says: *Howdy ma'am, sir*

20

the bus window frames a crowd
pressing a woman who has stolen a hat—
its tag dangles—pushing it in her face
two helmeted
police converge on her terror

21

the old man plunks down beside me and
launches into the Yiddish Art Theatre
Drama of his battle over the hydro bill
I cool him down with english

22

ten Hassidim march down our street in
fur-rimmed shtreimlach, waving banners, bearing
flares and torches to greet the Rebbeh
police cars lead and follow
it's kind of different, the cop admits

23

this is a dream: it is midnight
I put my head out of the window and see:
down my street where the young home-
steaders have grown old or died
and their hopscotch children skipped off
a brass band thumping oompah-tubas &
twirling majorettes
I think: *I've got to get out of the suburbs*

24

way down Spadina Avenue
merchandizing ideographs and blinking
neon diacritical marks
sell dim sum & bok choy where
once the rag trades sewed their sequined dresses
Come on, I'll outfit you from top to bottom
cousin Hymie said

25

on Eglinton west of Bathurst
at the Monte Carlo Restaurant
first time out after the operation
the waiter stares at the bones and says
You sure know how to eat a chicken

26

that old Chas Addams house on Lonsdale
Road shadowed and eerie in curlicued
gables was where bad-tempered
Professor Wadson lived, redfaced, sweet-
wived, a drinker of fine whiskey, but
where I live now at Lonsdale's other end
and watch the red moon rise I can't see
Wadson's house (he was young once, his
photo said, and handsome in Navy blues)
he's dead & gone now, & his whiskey all drunk up

27
straightback Yonge runs main and mighty
almost truly north to Hudson's Bay, but
striding parallel beyond his classy mistress Avenue
Road, it's Bathurst that's the Street of Life, she's
the farshlepta wife who guards
our spring and winter rituals, birth & death
hospital, church and synagogue, she's a

28
strong, ugly and no nonsense roadway rising
out of Toronto Harbour, no Venus either
among the boating not quite yachting clubs
using a swath of iron bridge to cross the
braided tracks of the railway yards past
factories and warehouses, pauses

29
here in the cancer ward at Western
the hospital I was born in: there's my
mother-in-law Jenny Bardikoff: *Poison and*
garbage they give you here in little roundy pills!
Better than the food! cries proper Mrs Scrimgeour
What a life we're living, Jenny!
cracking each other up joking to death

30

the eyeballs pop: Here's Honest Ed!
His lights are shining!
How we admire his sign's designing
with cheerful face he sells us trinkets & theatrics
and ever en famille in lamplit eateries
for modest sums we ate his steaks his peas,
his mashed potatoes
with not bad wines
and crusty waiters
So sparkle on at Bloor & Bathurst brightly!
We love you always, Ed! And not just lightly

31

this street that points to Dupont now
is homeliness of ailanthus, ginkos and red bricks
wrapped in trellised rose-bines, a
hologram chip of an old city's whole

32

the old woman sits down beside me on the bus
at Eglinton, quietly, this one
and I think: Manya? I'd met her
long ago in the hospital hoarding
the scraps of food, crust, half a potato
she'd been denied in Auschwitz. Her watch
has stopped. There was, there is no cure
for Manya's fifty-year disease of grief: *Eat salt,*
my mother said, *if you have nothing else.*
Eat salt.
Manya, is it you? I am so afraid
I let her get up and go without a word

33

foursquare flat-topped
Branson where we took her after she'd
slid along the road on her shoulder
ten feet back from that car's headlights   *Let her*
live, God! kept those dirty ragged clothes on the
living room book shelf until she came home

34

up at the Jewish Home
for the Aged, there are forty-odd
women on the patio sitting heads canted
& mouths agape except for
my mother in her wheelchair
Good sunny day, I say
Yeah, my mother says, *all the old*
flowers are out

35

drive, she said, up past Steeles, Bathurst
just skirting edges of green lawns, sweet flowers
past those synagogues, weddings made and broken,
vows taken and shattered, nights of lit candles
and memorials, past those wards of white beds and
trembling nights, past the strip malls where glatt
kosher & kosher style battle it out, past
Centennial where they've lifted him out of the snow and
sent him to heal

36
out farther yet and up
where if you are drifting
in a balloon at sunset
it is not quite like Hokusai seeing Fuji
through barrel hoops, among kite strings and
under the Great Wave
the city's swathed in haze, in its vision
not magic or majestic, it is a gathering
of human beings among the trees, it is the city

Geffen and Ravna: Four Sestinas

I

The men who brought the woman in for spying—
Ravna the Farroes, and barely a woman
they said—cast lots for her, men from levels
dark under, deep in the pits of the Station.
But Daniel Armsbearer gave her charge to Geffen
the Wardman, a choice that set those men to laughter

on that last outpost world where Terra Station
hardly called outward, least of all in laughter
to Farroes Colony. Nothing but skirmish and spying
between them over the broad snowfield, its levels
strata of rotted snow below lead sky. Geffen
the Wardman had never been known to need a woman.

And anyway, she was a Farroes woman,
alien, spined like a lizard, home in the cloud levels
and angled cells of a striated station,
who looked across at Terra onyx-eyed, spying
and skirmish her iron lovers. Geffen
listened to her captive voice, no laughter

there, in interrogation. Always other levels
of meaning rose in her words, like harmonics. A woman
of fine bones, muscular swift legs, spying
clumsily, angular alien in a Terra Station
with no secrets, for Farroes who did not need them. Geffen
did not consider this, not given to laughter.

Of spying, skirmish, levels, Station, Geffen
lifelong an unquestioner of levels
cared nothing; he looked and wanted Ravna, a woman
no matter how stark the tips of her spines. Spying?
No matter that, nor how much he stirred laughter
among fat whores or grizzled warriors in the firelit Station.

In those days of her captivity Ravna watched Geffen,
a thickhaired sombre man, seemed to be spying
even asleep with onyx eyes thin-lidded. Laughter
as strange to both as they to each other's levels,
laughter rolled always down the walls of the Station.
Sometimes it caused a trembling in the woman.

When Geffen felt air shivering around the woman
and heard laughter shattering off the levels
he damned skirmish and spying and every filthy station.

II

He waited out Ravna's presence for a word
spoken to him alone, her eyes direction:
for her thin narrow tongue to click with her light breath.
Then Daniel, a dishfaced man with sunken eyes,
said: "Days are shortening, and there's damned poor hunting."
She clenched her faintly patterned arms to her body

with a rasping of fingers over crèpy skin: the word
was of warriors who spent the summers hunting
leathery brooding beasts that grazed snow, breath
melting the frost over yellow groundleaf clumps, eyes
whiteblind sensing a warm dark direction.
She said, "Geffen, will they kill me?" hugging her body,

spines straining her robe's cord laces, the word
kill clicking against her small teeth with a breath
like a blade. His word. He looked in no direction
down smoky archways with cookpots steaming, eyes
sore with watching, soul dark with his sexual body.
"If they try, there'll be more than one for hunting."

Geffen was torn from his heavy dream over the breath
of prisoners in their night terrors, by a word
hissed: "Your serpent woman's gone whoring." His body
twitched from its thick sleep, but no direction
led to escape in Terra Station, where hunting
was short, and no game. Wardwoman Katrin's eyes
challenged. She tossed him his filched key. "What's the
word,Geffen? Shall I leave her to Daniel?"
                                        Ravna's body
stood tight. She was pinchbruised and out of breath,
her nails bloody from scratching at captors. Her eyes
knew no direction that was not death's direction.
Katrin laughed. "He might not think she's worth hunting."

"No. I will not deliver her."
                        Ravna's eyes
turned defiant.
            "Why'd you do that, woman?"
She spat. "What d'you care, you enemy? Hunting,
not whoring—isn't it—your direction.
and you're not Farroes, are you, with that body?
Are you?" A fall of icicles in a word.

"Farroes?" Her eyes were spears. His body
twinged cold, as if he'd caught the breath of hunting.
And he thought: *I have waited too long for a word.*

III

"Seven years ago we sent him to spy—and he's mine.
Trimmed off his spines, thickened his meat and bones
with drugs and strange foods, and trained him to forget
Farroes and be a thick fat lump of Earth.
We trained him too well; he has forgotten his people
and he has changed so far he might be, yes, you . . ."

She stood in the angles of her narrow bones.
A whisper: "We're leaving here, you see? I want what's mine.
I came and let the lewd-fingered of the Earth
pick over my body, because I don't forget
even if he means nothing to either people.
Geffen," a breath, "I want him to be you."

Geffen sweated cold. "It's easy for you
to want. I'm no betrayer. My people
are not Farroes, we're your fat lumps from Earth.
Get up, you! It's morning." He shook the racked bones
of wretches on plank beds. "These Farroes don't forget
where they come from, do they?" "No, but they're not mine."

Each hour the question weighed: *Geffen, is is you?*
I want him to be you.
                    Woman, you turn my bones
to water. However could I forget
you? She did not speak that day, but at night, "Mine,
Geffen, I want to know . . ." He raged: "If I am of Earth
I cannot love a woman of my people

and if I am Farroes, I'm outlandish. You say, *mine,*
mine! But I want firesides, meat and drink, my people
aren't Farroes from the cold levels where my bones
ache!" "Then take me to bed and let me judge you.
It is a small secret to keep. You will forget
it and me soon enough when you are back on Earth."

She fell silent, and was one of her people
again, a prisoner, one the gods forget.
When he put off his leather plates and rolled his bones
in his rough blankets he felt weak as a child, Earth
was far and alien. Her cool hand's touch: "Who are you
really, Geffen?" "Whoever, you are mine."

Her bones angled his angled arms. "I forget,"
he kissed the salt tips of her spines, "I forswear Earth's people
because Farroes is Paradise and you are mine."

IV

Geffen thought her smell was like flowers of snow
his hard scarred flesh could not melt. He called, *Ravna!*
in his dream because she seemed to be moving away
murmuring, *I will never find him before I die,*
and there were avenues of green trees but they were cold,
and something dark that he could not remember.

He woke to see her lying like a snow-
carved statue on her rack bed. He turned away.
Dread mantled him. He wrenched his mind to remember
anything of Farroes, anything of Ravna,
spent his free day at hunting, shivered with the cold
and, for the first time, to see a creature die.

He came from hunting heart-weary, with snow
in his beard. Daniel was cursing Katrin, and Ravna
gone."Not far from here, not far enough away,"
he whispered.
   "Then find her, Geffen." *I will die
before I find him.*
     *Yes, I will not remember
last night, or not for long.* Deep in the cold

and fireless levels, his lantern lit Ravna
enfolding a drunken gunner. He pulled her away
and kicked the man. She wept. Her skin was cold,
her bones thin. "Don't kill me, Geffen! Remember—"
"Nothing. You are a schemer and liar and you will die."
"It was no lie that I loved you, Geffen!" The snow

melted on him and he delivered her: to die
in the deep bed of the treacherous, the shroud of snow.
When he washed in hot cloths to turn the anguish away
the threads caught on his back's invisible scars *Ravna!*
and he remembered—he was forced to remember
their child's death, and their despair, and their cold.

He beat at the earth, coughed grief, and begged to die
until the breath bled in his throat.
                                    Ravna!
The rumour that he was Farroes faded away.
Some dream he went hunting and was tusked. Some remember,
or claim, he hung about tavern kitchens complaining of cold,
gnawing stale crusts with his wine. Or, that snow
claimed him, to die unfound.

                            Or: there was no Ravna,
no Geffen, only the baffled and weary drifting away
from a cold world where there are none left to remember.

AGMV Marquis

MEMBRE DE SCABRINI MEDIA

Québec, Canada
2002